101 Reasons Why I Love You!

Glen R. Landin

Copyright © 2015 Glen R. Landin.

No part of this publication may be reproduced or transmitted in any form or by any means, electronic or mechanical, including photocopying, recording, or by any information storage or retrieval system without written permission from the publisher.

CREATIVEARTISTIC PUBLISHING
ORANGE, CALIFORNIA

ISBN 978-0-692-37876-2

PRINTED EDITION: FEBRUARY 2015

PRINTED IN THE UNITED STATES OF AMERICA

WWW.GLENLANDIN.COM
WWW.CREATIVEARTISTICPUBLISHING.COM

GLEN R. LANDIN

101 Reasons Why I Love You!
is comprised of unique and creative reasons why someone falls truly in love with one another. The reasons contained in this book would be suitable for any true and loving relationship.

101 REASONS WHY I LOVE YOU!

GLEN R. LANDIN

101 REASONS WHY I LOVE YOU!

I Love You Because

Our communication flows

GLEN R. LANDIN

GLEN R. LANDIN

GLEN R. LANDIN

GLEN R. LANDIN

GLEN R. LANDIN

GLEN R. LANDIN

101 REASONS WHY I LOVE YOU!

GLEN R. LANDIN

101 REASONS WHY I LOVE YOU!

GLEN R. LANDIN

101 REASONS WHY I LOVE YOU!

GLEN R. LANDIN

GLEN R. LANDIN

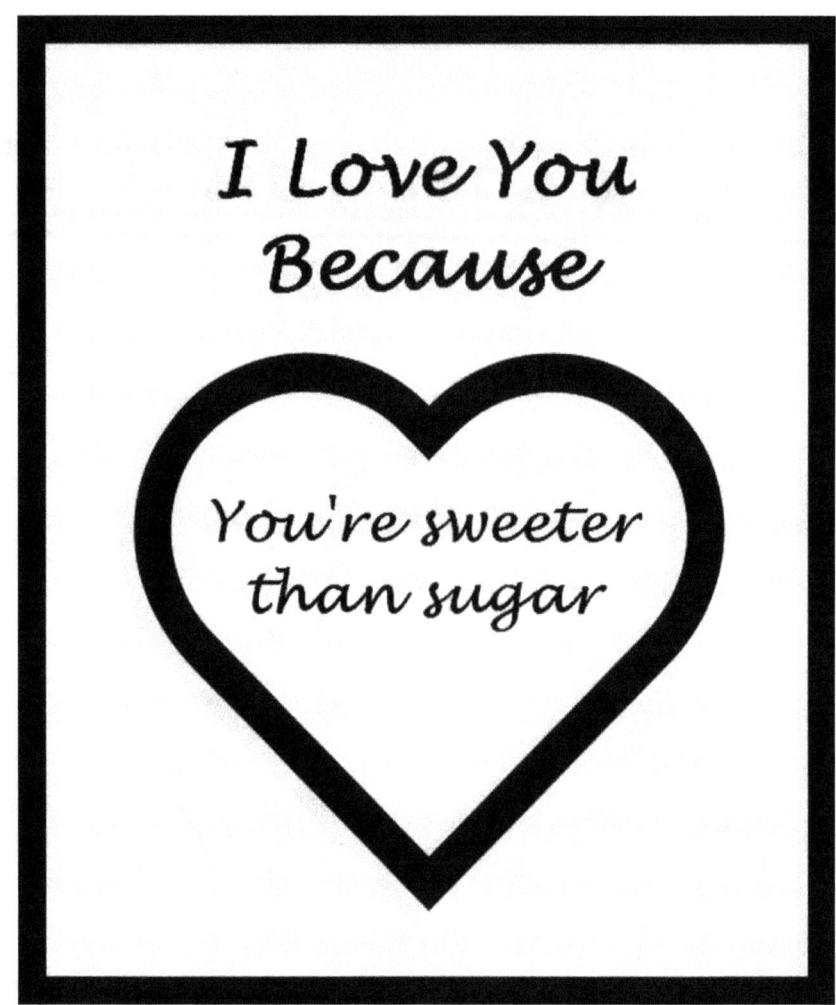

101 REASONS WHY I LOVE YOU!

GLEN R. LANDIN

I Love You Because

The romantic evenings

GLEN R. LANDIN

101 REASONS WHY I LOVE YOU!

I Love You Because

Our unique passions

GLEN R. LANDIN

GLEN R. LANDIN

GLEN R. LANDIN

GLEN R. LANDIN

101 REASONS WHY I LOVE YOU!

GLEN R. LANDIN

GLEN R. LANDIN

GLEN R. LANDIN

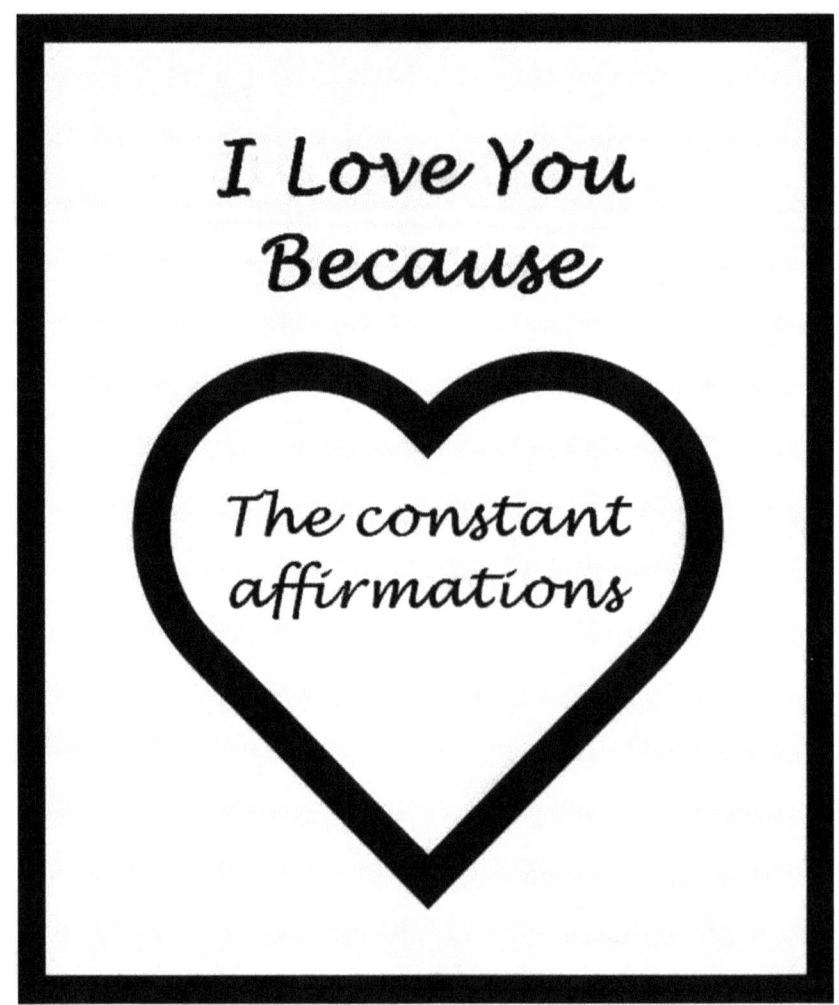

GLEN R. LANDIN

GLEN R. LANDIN

101 REASONS WHY I LOVE YOU!

GLEN R. LANDIN

GLEN R. LANDIN

101 REASONS WHY I LOVE YOU!

I Love You Because

Our ESP moments

GLEN R. LANDIN

101 REASONS WHY I LOVE YOU!

I Love You Because

We laugh together

GLEN R. LANDIN

GLEN R. LANDIN

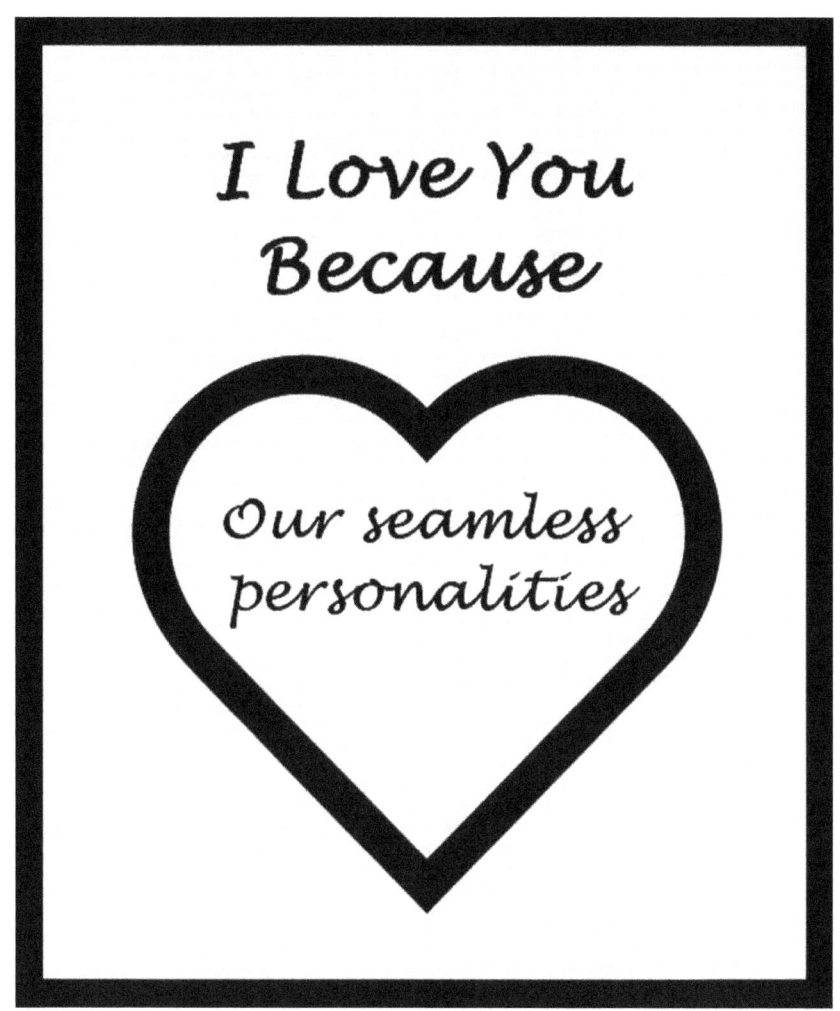

GLEN R. LANDIN

GLEN R. LANDIN

101 REASONS WHY I LOVE YOU!

GLEN R. LANDIN

GLEN R. LANDIN

GLEN R. LANDIN

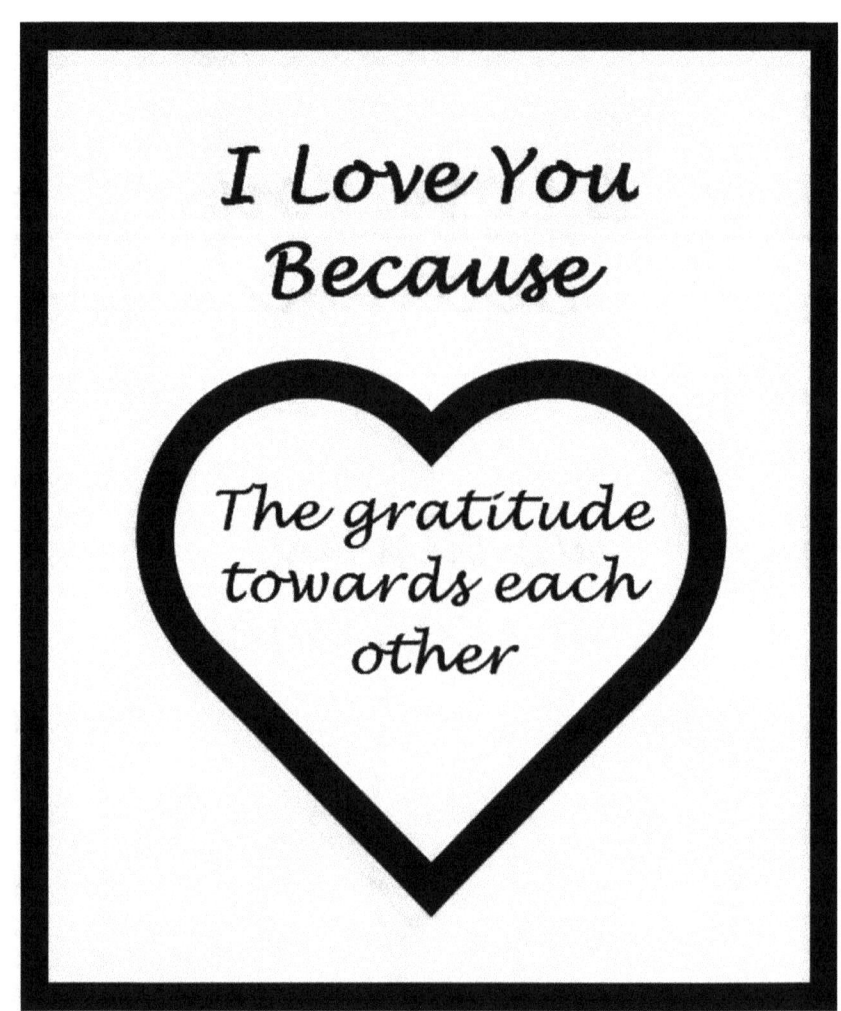

GLEN R. LANDIN

GLEN R. LANDIN

GLEN R. LANDIN

101 REASONS WHY I LOVE YOU!

GLEN R. LANDIN

GLEN R. LANDIN

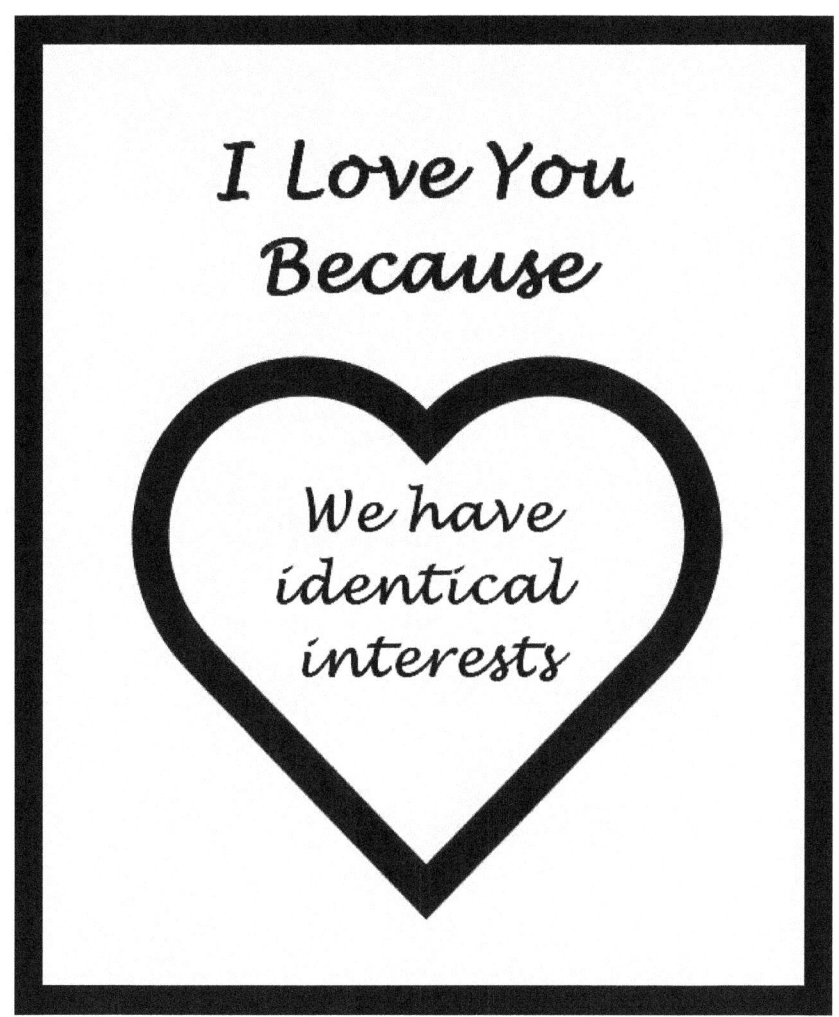

GLEN R. LANDIN

GLEN R. LANDIN

GLEN R. LANDIN

GLEN R. LANDIN

GLEN R. LANDIN

GLEN R. LANDIN

GLEN R. LANDIN

101 REASONS WHY I LOVE YOU!

GLEN R. LANDIN

101 REASONS WHY I LOVE YOU!

GLEN R. LANDIN

GLEN R. LANDIN

GLEN R. LANDIN

101 REASONS WHY I LOVE YOU!

101

GLEN R. LANDIN

About The Author

Glen Landin continues writing unique and informative books. In this release entitled, "101 Reasons Why I Love You!" he combines the most simple, unique and creative reasons to love someone and includes a large silhouette heart on each page.

As a creative writer and author, Glen also enjoys interior design, photography, model railroading, visual displays, and traveling to nearby and distant shores.

Through Glen's creative writing skills, using poems, phrases, affirmations, and messages, he inspires, encourages, and motivates people to simply believe in yourself. Because all things are possible to those who believe!

www.ingramcontent.com/pod-product-compliance
Lightning Source LLC
Chambersburg PA
CBHW071720040426
42446CB00011B/2142